# By Charles Simic

## *TRANSLATIONS*

## *ANTHOLOGY*

# DISMANTLING
# THE
# SILENCE

For Peter and Jean

Charlie

Nov 18, 1992

# DISMANTLING THE SILENCE

Poems by

## CHARLES SIMIC

*with a note by Richard Howard*

GEORGE BRAZILLER

*New York*

Some of these poems have previously appeared in the following publications, to whose editors grateful acknowledgment is made: *Chelsea, Chicago Review, Hearse, The Iowa Review, Kayak, New American and Canadian Poetry, New Work, Lillabulero, Poetry, Stony Brook, Sumac,* and *Xenia.*

The author also wishes to thank the following publishers for permission to reprint poems which have previously appeared in broadside or book: Unicorn Press, Kayak Press, and Sumac Press.

*Standard Book Number: 0-8076-0590-5*
*Library of Congress Card Number: 79-143397*
*Fifth Printing, April 1984*
*Designed by Harry Ford and Kathleen Carey*
*Printed in the United States of America*

*For Her*

# *Contents*

# III

# IV

# V

# CHARLES SIMIC

*"My voice now the mad captain thrown in chains*
*by his suffering crew."*

It is a delight to initiate this series of poetry publications with Charles Simic's first full collection, but not a discovery. Had George Hitchcock not brought out Mr. Simic's earlier work in the last four years, had two of his fellow poets not commended that work to the editor of this series, even so it could not be said that the poet has been discovered, for no poet is discovered. A poet discovers himself, or better still, is discovered by himself, by that other self which stretches away from him in the form of his poems:

> Though you utter
> Every one of my words,
> You are a stranger.
> It's time you spoke.

So speaks Charles Simic who, after the study of Michaux and the French surrealists on the one hand and of the American plains poets on the other, discovered Roethke—for one *can* discover *other* poets for oneself. And in the poetry which he has written since these eminences and influences were assimilated or disclaimed, since his exposure in his own person, as a soldier, to precisely the Eastern Europe from which he derives, I should prefer to say that Simic has been not only discovered by himself but *recovered*, for *Dismantling the Silence* reinstates an ancient wisdom, as well as an ancient fooling, which, by its presence, we suddenly realize has been absent from recent American verse—a gnomic utterance, convinced in accent, collective in reference, original in impulse.

When we speak of writing as *original*, as I am bound and determined to do in speaking of Charles Simic's writing at all, we mean that it has to do with something very old, not something very new—it has to do with origins, beginnings, sources. Simic's poems come to us from a much hoarier age than the mere biography of the poet warrants (he is thirty-two); they come to us, for all the immense care he has taken to speak freshly and boldly and withal modestly "that these words may step out of their winter"—they come to us, then, from an enormous otherness, a distance beyond words, wrought out of remote elements of the imagination of hinterlands, a diction tinged with menace and with grotesquerie: "I sat between the word *obscure* and the word *gallows*." These poems are written, and must be heard, "in a voice to equal the silence that surrounds it."

Displacing the familiar until it turns primitive once again, and because these poems reach us from another region, it would seem, where all things are taken in the image of our flesh ("the human body will be revealed for what it is")—the world the content of our bodies, then, and not our bodies merely abiding the world—they often assume the resonance of lessons, litanies, manuals, catalogues, bestiaries, parodies of that old wisdom-literature by which men once kept their minds on the world. Except for the very last poem in this book (and it is called "*erratum*"), there are no other people here, though there are presences and there are processes (the wind, a field, fear, spiderwebs); in Simic's poetry we do not concern or belong to each other or even ourselves, but to our objects—shoes, food—which know our bodies as only the spoon can know the mouth. "I am whatever beast inhabits me," he asserts, he exults, and in another place: "it is not only its own life that man's body has to endure." Exile as homecoming, then, and the natural world accepted as a celebration, a rite, however sinister; identity will be dispossessed until, as Simic prophesies in one of the best definitions of poetry I know, "the ear will crawl back into the eye."

I spoke of these poems as reaching us from a distance beyond words, and indeed so abrupt, so *unheard-of* are the images, which Simic's scrupulous rhythms slide unopposed into our minds, that they seem, at first, not to have been made of language at all. They seem merely—merely!—something we shall know always, though we never could have known it before. And so they are, though it has all been done with words, words spoken out of a silence, into a silence:

> This is a tale with a kernel.
> You'll have to use your own teeth to crack it.

RICHARD HOWARD

I

# FOREST

My time is coming. Once again
My trees will swing their heavy bells.

My termites, my roots and streams
Will stitch their chill into the heart of man
Laying out my most ancient trail.

I speak of the north, of its pull
Stuck in my mouth like a bit.

Whoever looks now in the palm of his hand
Will notice the imprints of strange flowers
I have preserved in my rocks.

I will bare bones to tell fortunes by,
Snow with tracks of all the fabled highwaymen.
Ladies and gentlemen, you will hear a star
Dead a million years, in the throat of a bird.

The human body will be revealed for what it is—
A cluster of roots
Pulling in every direction.

There'll be plenty of time
When an acorn grows out of your ear
To accustom yourself to my ways,
To carve yourself a hermit's toothpick.

# THE WIND

Touching me, you touch
The country that has exiled you.

# POEM

Every morning I forget how it is.
I watch the smoke mount
In great strides above the city.
I belong to no one.

Then, I remember my shoes,
How I have to put them on,
How bending over to tie them up
I will look into the earth.

# PASTORAL

I came to a field
Where the grass was silence
And flowers
Words

I saw they were both
Of flesh and blood
And that they sense and fear
The wind like a knife

So I sat between the word *obscure*
And the word *gallows*
Took out my small cauldron
And ladle

Whistled to the word *fire*
And she answered me
From her sleep

Spat in the palm of my hand
To catch the stars
Behind my back
And light her way

# DISMANTLING THE SILENCE

Take down its ears first
Carefully so they don't spill over.
With a sharp whistle slit its belly open.
If there are ashes in it, close your eyes
And blow them whichever way the wind is pointing.
If there's water, sleeping water,
Bring the root of a plant that hasn't drunk for a month.

When you reach the bones,
And you haven't got a pack of dogs with you,
And you haven't got a pine coffin
And a wagon pulled by oxen to make them rattle,
Slip them quickly under your skin,
Next time you pick up your sack,
You'll hear them setting your teeth on edge. . .

It is now completely dark.
Slowly and with patience
Feel its heart. You will need to haul
A heavy chest of drawers
Into its emptiness
To make it creak
On its wheel.

# SUMMER MORNING

I love to stretch
Like this, naked
On my bed in the morning;
Quiet, listening:

Outside they are opening
Their primers
In the little school
Of the cornfield.

There is a smell of damp hay,
Of horses, of summer sky,
Of laziness, of eternal life.

I know all the dark places
Where the sun hasn't reached yet,
Where the singing has just ceased
In the hidden aviaries of the crickets—
Anthills where it goes on raining—
Slumbering spiders dreaming of wedding dresses.

I pass over the farmhouses
Where the little mouths open to suck,
Barnyards where a man, naked to the waist,
Washes his face with a hose,
Where the dishes begin to rattle in the kitchen.

The good tree with its voice
Of a mountain brook
Knows my steps
It hushes.

I stop and listen:
Somewhere close by
A stone cracks a knuckle,
Another turns over in its sleep.

I hear a butterfly stirring
In the tiny soul of the caterpillar.
I hear the dust dreaming
Of eyes and great winds.

Further ahead, someone
Even more silent
Passes over the grass
Without bending it.

—And all of a sudden
In the midst of that silence
It seems possible
To live simply
On the earth.

# TO ALL HOG-RAISERS, MY ANCESTORS

When I eat pork, it's solemn business.
I am eating my ancestors.
I am eating the land they worked on.

Turnip-headed drunks, horse-thieves,
Lechers, brutes, filthy laborers,
I revive you within my blood.

If I add garlic to my pork
It is for one who became a minister,
Who left the land, city-bound,
Changed his name, never to be heard of again.

# FEAR

Fear passes from man to man
Unknowing,
As one leaf passes its shudder
To another.

All at once the whole tree is trembling
And there is no sign of the wind.

# SPIDER

Teacher of Swedenborg and St. John of the Cross,
First anchorite, mysterious builder—
From the dark corner of my room
His destination
The distant northern star. . .

As he weaves, as he spreads his webs,
He is singing.
I'm certain of it,
He is singing.

# EVENING

The snail gives off stillness.
The weed is blessed.
At the end of a long day
The man finds joy, the water peace.

Let all be simple. Let all stand still
Without a final direction.
That which brings you into the world
To take you away at death
Is one and the same;
The shadow long and pointy
Is its church.

At night some understand what the grass says.
The grass knows a word or two.
It is not much. It repeats the same word
Again and again, but not too loudly . . .

Toward evening
When it stops snowing
Our homes rise
High above the earth
Into that soundless space
Where neither the bark of a dog
Nor the cry of a bird reaches.

We are like the ancient seamen:
Our bodies are the ocean
And the silence is the boat
God has provided
For our long and unknown journey.

# HUNGER

We are old friends.
She put my father to bed
When he was little.

Her stories are like lace
The girls from the last century
Wore against their thighs.

There are dogs
Who want to bite her throat.
No use. There isn't a grain
Of salt in it.

The old lady
Makes jams.
For recipe she takes the palm
From a newborn child.

Take it as a medicine,
A teaspoon at a time, and remember:
You are a Saint turned over on a spit,
You are a roach caught by the convicts.

When you can't get out of bed
She'll come visiting
In her white bonnet
Tapping her cane.

With a tiny silver spoon
She'll part the bark of your lips.
She's a bee, you are her flower.
That's all the explanation I find necessary.

I'm going to lie down next to you.
It cannot grow colder than this hour.
Strange men are gathered again
Drinking and singing. A different young man
Sits in their midst dressed in a uniform.

We are well into the night. Black moon.
With candle and spoon they examine its mouth.
A man with dead soul and dog-licked knuckles
Eats from a paper plate.

I'm going to lie down next to you
As if nothing has happened:
Boot, shoemaker's knife, woman,
Your point bearing to my heart's true north.

*

This is a tale with a kernel.
You'll have to use your own teeth to crack it.

If not tonight, well then . . . tomorrow.
Who keeps a clear head,
Who doesn't take a nap . . .
There isn't much choice anyway,
It's too late to get your money back.

All I can say at this point—
You won't have to kiss anyone's ass,
Nor will you have to sign anything.
It will all take place on the quiet
The way love is made.

*

A sound of wings doesn't mean there's a bird.
If you've eaten today, no reason to think you'll eat tomorrow.
People can also be processed into soap.
The trees rustle. There's not always someone to answer them.
Moon hound of the north you come barking you come barking.
It's not only its own life that man's body has to endure.

\*

WANTED: A needle swift enough
To sew this poem into a blanket.

# SLEEP

The woodpecker goes beating a little drum.
The shadow of the hyena blackens my face.
In my legs which are to be judged harshly,
And my hands with their false fury,
The bones lull each other tenderly.
I am with all that shivers,
All that hangs limp and without life.

It rains toads. My blood runs
Past dark inner cities on fire.
I climb into deep wells,
Rock bottoms and bone bottoms
Where gall of my birth steams.

Things slip out of my grasp,
Other things come to a quiet end.
This is my song. Nothing of us remains.
Almost nothing. I am whatever beast inhabits me.

When the rain turns into snow
Every beast shall see its track and wonder.

# II

# THE ANIMALS

I have no news of the animals.
Do they still exist? Those toads
I used to know so well. And the foxes,
Are they still out there in the dark?

Impossible. Where a horse used to graze
In my dream—an emptiness, edge of a cliff
On which I balance myself
With no skill and plenty of luck.

I can see now that I'll have to construct
My bestiary in some other manner:
Without a bone or an eye,
Without even a track of blood in the snow,
And the barking
Reaching over my shoulders.

Alone, without a model—
It will be up to me
To imagine, out of the stones and debris
That are left, a new species—

A tooth,
An udder
Full of milk.

# BUTCHER SHOP

Sometimes walking late at night
I stop before a closed butcher shop.
There is a single light in the store
Like the light in which the convict digs his tunnel.

An apron hangs on the hook:
The blood on it smeared into a map
Of the great continents of blood,
The great rivers and oceans of blood.

There are knives that glitter like altars
In a dark church
Where they bring the cripple and the imbecile
To be healed.

There is a wooden slab where bones are broken,
Scraped clean:—a river dried to its bed
Where I am fed,
Where deep in the night I hear a voice.

# BONES

My roof is covered with pigeon bones.
I do not disturb them. I leave them
Where they are, warm
In their beds of feathers.

At night I think I hear the bones,
The little skulls cracking against the tin,
For the wind is blowing softly, so softly,
As if a cricket were singing inside a tulip. . .

What is joy to me is grief to others.
I feel grief all around my house
Like a ring of beasts circling a camp fire
Before dawn.

# MEAT

## 1

Hang the meat on the hook
So that I may see what I am.
Hang that dying pig,
I want to see breath shake off
The heaviness of the flesh

## 2

Scalded, guts cleaned,
The pig hangs.
The heaviness of it
Like the weight of a man
Who has turned to go
With grief in his heart.

## 3

I am baptized in this sight,
As when a child immersed in water
Feels the hand of death
At his throat.

# LAST SUPPER

The teeth are first to come:
Two that were always left hungry.
The ears follow gloomily behind
Balancing themselves on stilts.

Then the eye arrives:
One millionth of an inch
Of pure longing.

The bones are already at the table:
White, delicate as maidenheads,
Their halos in place
Each hung by a meat hook.

The blood by now should be in the cups,
The hairs are making conversation.

There's also something trampled:
Tongue or tail it's hard to tell.
It snores under the table waiting for leftovers.

The one they are all waiting for
Is the last to sit down.
As he breaks this bandit's heart
Into thirteen morsels,
His throat swells:

He's a lunar rooster
Whose crow doesn't reach.

# THE INNER MAN

It isn't the body
That's a stranger.
It's someone else.

We poke the same
Ugly mug
At the world.
When I scratch,
He scratches too.

There are women
Who claim to have held him.
A dog follows me about.
It might be his.

If I'm quiet, he's quieter.
So I forget him.
Yet, as I bend down
To tie my shoelaces,
He's standing up.

We cast a single shadow.
Whose shadow?

I'd like to say:
"He was in the beginning
And he'll be in the end,"
But one can't be sure.

At night
As I sit
Shuffling the cards of our silence,
I say to him:

"Though you utter
Every one of my words,
You are a stranger.
It's time you spoke."

# HEARING STEPS

Someone is walking through the snow:
An ancient sound. Perhaps the Mongols are migrating again?
Perhaps, once more we'll go hanging virgins
From bare trees, plundering churches,
Raping widows in the deep snow?

Perhaps, the time has come again
To go back into forests and snow fields,
Live alone killing wolves with our bare hands,
Until the last word and the last sound
Of this language I am speaking is forgotten.

# TAPESTRY

It hangs from heaven to earth.
There are trees in it, cities, rivers,
small pigs and moons. In one corner
snow is falling over a charging cavalry,
in another women are planting rice.

You can also see:
a chicken carried off by a fox,
a naked couple on their wedding night,
a column of smoke,
an evil-eyed woman spitting into a pail of milk.

What is behind it?
—Space, plenty of empty space.

And who is talking now?
—A man asleep under a hat.

And when he wakes up?
—He'll go into the barbershop.
They'll shave his beard, nose, ears and hair
To look like everyone else.

# PSALM

### 1

Old ones to the side.

If there's a tailor, let him sit
With his legs crossed.
My suit will arrive in a moment.

All priests into mouse-holes.
All merchants into pigs. We'll cut their throats later.

To the beggars a yawn,
We'll see how they'll climb into it.

To the one who thinks, to the one between yes and no,
A pound of onions to peel.

To the mad ones crowns, if they still want them.
To the soldier a manual to turn into a flea.

No one is to touch the children.
No one is to shovel out the dreamers.

### 2

I'm Joseph of the Joseph of the Joseph who rode on a donkey,
A wind-mill on the tongue humming with stars,
Columbus himself chained to a chair,
I'm anyone looking for a broom-closet.

### 3

You must understand that I write this at night
Their sleep surrounds me like an ocean.
Her name is Mary, the most mysterious of all.
She's a forest, standing at the beginning of time.
I'm someone lying within it. This light is our sperm.
The forest is old, older than sleep,
Older than this psalm I'm singing right to the end.

# MARCHING

After I forgot about the horses
And when the fire turned into cool water flowing,
And the old woman took off her mourning to enter a coffin
At the end of a long life

A horse stood like an apparition,
A dream of a drowned girl cast out by the sea,
Suddenly he turned his head, bugler turning his bugle
To face the moon shining like a newlaid egg.

Then I rose in my house among my sons,
I put on my old clothes and my muddy boots,
My clothes smelling of wolves and deep snow,
My boots that have trodden men's faces.

I remembered the swamps, grass taller than horses,
Fast rivers softer than chicken flesh,
Where I'll stumble into deep hollows, dark eyelids,
Until I am buried under human droppings.

Blood rose into my head shaking its little bells.
In the valley the glow died in the udder of the cow.
The trees ceased playing with their apples
And the wind brought the sound of men marching.

A dog went along the road in front of marching soldiers,
A man who was to be hanged went along the road,
His head was bent, his face was dark and twisted
As if death meant straining to empty one's bowels.

So close the doors and windows and do not look,
The stars will come into the autumn sky
Like boats looking for survivors at sea
But no son of yours will rise from the deep.

# FOR THE VICTIMS

*to Michael Benedikt*

The worst is still to come
When the blackness creeps out of milk
And the stone coughs up its secret pit
Which will prove to be just another stone,

And this old board lets out a yell
Which it held since the time it was still a seed,
A yell more like a sudden light
Than a sound,

And this chair will reveal itself
As the exact shadow of someone
Who stood here all this time
So that these words may step out of their winter
Or grains of salt (it's the same thing).

I say nothing of crows cawing
And the language of rustling grasses
But there'll be plenty of that,
Plus the roar of the ocean,
Its obscure aphorism spelled out—

Then, at last, we'll get a true taste of ourselves.
The ear will crawl back into the eye
Like Jonah into his whale.

When the knife beds down in the flesh
And flows away with the blood,
The anchor that keeps you in this old life
Will be lifted.

In any case, it's only an instant
That you have to worry about. The body
Will rise from the floor like a soap-bubble
To fall back with its old familiar thud.

# ANATOMY LESSON

We have before us
A magician's coffin
Sawn in half
With a girl in it

A knuckle knocking on wood
For its lips to be read
A heap of sucked wish-bones
Snoring on a plate

A bridge
Over nothing in particular
A stone that thinks
Itself a flower

A period a careless dot
After what sentence
A void big enough
For the universe
To make its kennel in it

A miner's lamp
That sooner or later
Will attract
Its own bullet

Hair and twenty nails
That go on growing
After its final
And absolute extinction

That is all

I leave you with
A door you don't wish to open
A key you are afraid to possess

A sound of jailer's boots

A voice that wanted
To equal the silence
That surrounds it

# EATING OUT THE ANGEL OF DEATH

*to Carl*

### I

Now my body is the evening sky
And I'm the smoke rising towards it,

Slowly since I watch for the wind,
Carefully, since I'm blind
And my dog and cane have been taken away.

I hear gnashing: those bones are afraid.
They imagine a raven: a lethal speck of summer.

I'm like a cold glass of milk
The stars will drink before going to bed.

O there's nothing more beautiful than this climb
With its bearded, haggard and open fist
Like the last barbarian
On the border of an invisible empire.

## 2

I'm back in your greasy kettle.
Lock me in with your crooked spoon.
Use me in place of ashes
To rub yourself with.

I'll curl down on the bottom
In my heavy coat of smoke
With an apple in each pocket,
Carnation in the buttonhole.

Together we'll watch our parents:
Father-fire carving himself a travelling stick,
Mother-water muttering the endless rosary
Of all that the stones took from her.

### 3

I'm searching
For what my left hand
Hid secretly
From the right:

Everything that my teeth ground in sleep,
The last hole on the flute of solitude,
All the kettle's orphans,
My messkit of time,
My ration of madness.

You can't have any of it.

When they peel off these covers
You'll see all that grew here in the dark:
The numb, heavy-breasted idol
I've kneaded of ear-wax.

## 4

Something goes through the world
Without speaking to anyone.
When it falls in water
It doesn't splash, when it enters a tree
It doesn't rustle.

The less you hear it the fiercer its presence is.
Time stops. There's a mist in the north
And a branch, only one branch pointing to it.
No creature may now share its stillness.

Cloud, drifting in the direction of my birth,
If there's a hell,
It must have only one inhabitant.

## 5

I come to put a bridle on you.
Stand still mongrel.
I have hundred different reins, straps.
They all stink of mud and branding irons.

My saddles are old, they speak
With holes where their jewels were ripped.
The hungry ones cooked them in their soups.

I have also whips and living spurs.
All fit you perfectly, only
When I mount you, my feet drag in the grass.

My white, baker's feet stick out
Like two ears in some other hell.

## 6

Our church on the tip of the nose
Let us take its dizzying host.

A black thought serves
On the altar of the open eye.

Let us kneel pinch of nothing
And pray sliver of pain.

To confess our brotherhood scum
From which the bones stitch their rags.

Our kettle of flying-carpets and carrion
From which the smoke laughs at night.

My voice now the mad captain
Thrown in chains by his suffering crew.

## 7

We shall ride out at daybreak.
We lived in its nearness a long time.
It was a house of a rich man
Surrounded by a high wall. We knew
It had a daughter who was very beautiful.
She slept in beds covered with lace
And washed her breasts in spring water.

We shall ride out at daybreak
Singing
On the narrow road
That passes under her window.

# IV

# TABLE

A little quiet, a little light
For us to sit at this table.

You pigheaded, you meat running from a slaughterhouse,
You nails that came out of the wall to catch a dove.

All that your night carried into mine,
All that my day carried into yours.

Here are two plates, an eye of a blindman
Alights on my finger, then four more.

To bang our fists on the table,
For the wood to answer hoarsely.

To shuffle our greasy pack of cards
With what chill is left in our bones.

This table is a raft sinking
With its cluster of galley-slaves.

This table is a cup I lift
Filled to the brim with dead stars.

To lay the dead man against its hardness.
Mine today, yours tomorrow.

To return then each into his own grain, his own knot,
For the grains and knots in this wood
To begin humming on their spindles.

# BESTIARY FOR THE FINGERS
## OF MY RIGHT HAND

### 1

Thumb, loose tooth of a horse.
Rooster to his hens.
Horn of a devil. Fat worm
They have attached to my flesh
At the time of my birth.
It takes four to hold him down,
Bend him in half, until the bone
Begins to whimper.

Cut him off. He can take care
Of himself. Take root in the earth,
Or go hunting with wolves.

### 2

The second points the way.
True way. The path crosses the earth,
The moon and some stars.
Watch, he points further.
He points to himself.

### 3

The middle one has backache.
Stiff, still unaccustomed to this life;
An old man at birth. It's about something
That he had and lost,
That he looks for within my hand,
The way a dog looks
For fleas
With a sharp tooth.

### 4

The fourth is mystery.
Sometimes as my hand
Rests on the table
He jumps by himself
As though someone called his name.

After each bone, finger,
I come to him, troubled.

### 5

Something stirs in the fifth
Something perpetually at the point
Of birth. Weak and submissive,
His touch is gentle.
It weighs a tear.
It takes the mote out of the eye.

# THE SPOON

An old spoon
Bent, gouged,
Polished to an evil
Glitter.

It has bitten
Into my life—
This kennel-bone
Sucked thin.

Now, it is a living
Thing: ready
To scratch a name
On a prison wall—

Ready to be passed on
To the little one
Just barely
Beginning to walk.

# FORK

This strange thing must have crept
Right out of hell.
It resembles a bird's foot
Worn around the cannibal's neck.

As you hold it in your hand,
As you stab with it into a piece of meat,
It is possible to imagine the rest of the bird:
Its head which like your fist
Is large, bald, beakless and blind.

# KNIFE

### 1

Father-confessor
Of the fat hen
On the red altar
Of its throat,

A tongue,
All alone,
Bearing the darkness of a mouth
Now lost.

A single shining eye
Of a madman—
If there's a tear in it,
Who is it for?

### 2

It is a candle
It is also a track
Of crooked letters;
The knife's mysterious writings.

We go down
An inner staircase.
We walk under the earth.
The knife lights the way.

Through bones of animals,
Water, beard of a wild boar—
We go through stones, embers,
We are after a scent.

### 3

So much darkness
Everywhere.
We are in a bag
Slung
Over someone's shoulders.

You hear the sound
Of marching boots.
You hear the earth
Answering
With a hollow thud.

If it's a poem
You want,
Take a knife;

A star of solitude,
It will rise and set in your hand.

# MY SHOES

Shoes, secret face of my inner life:
Two gaping toothless mouths,
Two partly decomposed animal skins
Smelling of mice-nests.

My brother and sister who died at birth
Continuing their existence in you,
Guiding my life
Toward their incomprehensible innocence.

What use are books to me
When in you it is possible to read
The Gospel of my life on earth
And still beyond, of things to come?

I want to proclaim the religion
I have devised for your perfect humility
And the strange church I am building
With you as the altar.

Ascetic and maternal, you endure:
Kin to oxen, to Saints, to condemned men,
With your mute patience, forming
The only true likeness of myself.

# STONE

Go inside a stone
That would be my way.
Let somebody else become a dove
Or gnash with a tiger's tooth.
I am happy to be a stone.

From the outside the stone is a riddle:
No one knows how to answer it.
Yet within, it must be cool and quiet
Even though a cow steps on it full weight,
Even though a child throws it in a river;
The stone sinks, slow, unperturbed
To the river bottom
Where the fishes come to knock on it
And listen.

I have seen sparks fly out
When two stones are rubbed,
So perhaps it is not dark inside after all;
Perhaps there is a moon shining
From somewhere, as though behind a hill—
Just enough light to make out
The strange writings, the star-charts
On the inner walls.

# STONE INSIDE A STONE

They will not turn into seed.
On the border of nothing and nothing.

Fossils of the wind.
But what wind?

You can't step twice in the same river—
With a stone you can take your sweet time.

Going to pick a flower in its heart
Is like taking a live chicken out of a bottle.

My stones will not sing the song yours are singing.

They say: everything is so simple. Touch it.
You awake in one, fall asleep in another.

Who, while the night is still deep, awakes the roosters?
A stone among us is taking notes.

The opposite has ceased to be imaginary.
There are two of us now but o what solitude.

## 2

Touch again. You've touched a lightning.
The thunder is still to come.

Once in my hand
The fingers speak to it in its own language.

Stone, you come from a long line of fire-thieves.
I answered your questions
Until your hardness entered my voice.
Now they can carve whatever tool they please.

This is bread never-sown, never-reaped.

Two of them hang in death's testicles.

Strength that wishes to contract
Until it resembles itself more fully.

I hear the steps of the stone.
I lift them with my tongue
To keep myself in shape
For an unknown time.

# POEM WITHOUT A TITLE

I say to the lead
Why did you let yourself
Be cast into a bullet?
Have you forgotten the alchemists?
Have you given up hope
Of turning into gold?

Nobody answers.
Lead. Bullet. With names
Such as these
The sleep is deep and long.

# A X

Whoever swings an ax
Knows the body of man
Will again be covered with fur.
The stench of blood and swamp water
Will return to its old resting place.
They'll spend their winters
Sleeping like the bears.
The skin on the breasts of their women
Will grow coarse. He who cannot
Grow teeth, will not survive.
He who cannot howl
Will not find his pack . . .

These dark prophecies were gathered,
Unknown to myself, by my body
Which understands historical probabilities,
Lacking itself, in its essence, a future.

# NEEDLE

### 1

Watch out for the needle,
She's the scent of a plant
The root of which is far and hidden.

She's the straw
From the nest
Where the blindfolded hand of your mother
Shelters her eggs.

She went out hunting
With your fathers in the old days.

Watch out for the emptiness
At the end of each of her tales,
The place where only a moment ago
She squinted.

### 2

Thread through her eye:
Two secret thoughts
A hair dipped in the ink of a spider
The silence of certain colors.

Stitch then that hole
Yawning toothless
From the back
Of my hanging shirt.

You'll hear the sound
Of nails growing
On sleeping men.

### 3

Do you keep losing your needles?
Tie in a handkerchief
A little salt, a little smoke,
It's time that you go looking for them.

When your little finger gets lost
In a forest, so that those
Who come later find only its ring
With thorns grown from the gold,
Know that you are near.

Close your eyes then.
If the needles open their doors,
They'll blind you.


### 4

Whenever a needle gets lost
She makes a perfect circle.
Her small eye becomes even smaller.

The match lit for her dies
In a noose of smoke. Every thread in the world
Turns black. The bent back of your mother
Is now an ancient stone.

Now under all that is soft,
Mellow and yielding,
Her sharp little tongue lies awake.

By and by
She'll make you shout
In your dream.

# EXPLORERS

They arrive inside
The object at evening.
There's no one to meet them.

The lamps they carry
Cast their shadows
Back into themselves.

They make notations:
The sky and the earth
Are of the same impenetrable color.
There's no wind. If there are rivers,
They must be under the ground.
Of the marvels we sought, no trace.
Of the strange new stars, nothing.
There's not even dust, so we must conclude
That someone passed recently
With a broom. . .

As they write, the tiny universe
Stitches its black thread into them.

Eventually nothing is left
Except a faint voice
Which might belong
Either to one of them
Or to someone who came before.

It says: I'm grateful
That you've finally come.
It was starting to get lonely.
I recognize you. You are all
That has eluded me.

May this be my country.

# CONCERNING MY NEIGHBORS,
## THE HITTITES

Great are the Hittites.
Their ears have mice and mice have holes.
Their dogs bury themselves and leave the bones
To guard the house. A single weed holds all their storms
Until the spiderwebs spread over the heavens.
There are bits of straw in their lakes and rivers
Looking for drowned men. When a camel won't pass
Through the eye of one of their needles,
They tie a house to its tail. Great are the Hittites.
Their fathers are in cradles, their newborn make war.
To them lead floats, a leaf sinks. Their god is the size
Of a mustard seed so that he can be quickly eaten.

They also piss against the wind,
Pour water in a leaky bucket,
Strike two tears to make fire,
And have tongues with bones in them,
Bones of a wolf gnawed by lambs.

\*

They are also called mound-builders,
They are called Asiatic horses
That will drink on the Rhine, they are called
My grandmother's fortune telling, they are called
You can't take it to the grave with you.

It's that hum in your left ear,
A sigh coming from deep within you,
A dream in which you keep falling forever,
The hour in which you sit up in bed
As though someone has shouted your name.

No one knows why the Hittites exist,
Still, when two are whispering
One of them is listening.

*

Did they catch the falling knife?
They caught it like a fly with closed mouths.
Did they balance the last egg?
They struck the egg with a bone so it won't howl.
Did they wait for dead man's shoes?
The shoes went in at one ear and out the other.
Did they wipe the blood from their mousetraps?
They burnt the blood to warm themselves.
Are they cold with no pockets in their shrouds?
If the sky falls they shall have clouds for supper.

What do they have for us
To put in our pipes and smoke?
They have the braid of a beautiful girl
That drew a team of cattle
And the engraving of him who slept
With dogs and rose with fleas
Searching for its trace in the sky.

*

And so there are fewer and fewer of them now.
Who wrote their name on paper
And burnt the paper? Who put snake-bones
In their pillows? Who threw nail-parings
In their soup? Who made them walk

69

Under the ladder? Who stuck pins
In their snapshots?

The wart of warts and his brother evil-eye.
Bone-lazy and her sister rabbit's-foot.
Cross-your-fingers and their father dogstar.
Knock-on-wood and his mother hell-fire.

Because the tail can't wag the cow.
Because the woods can't fly to the dove.
Because the stones haven't said their last word.
Because dunghills rise and empires fall.

*

They are leaving behind
All the silver spoons
Found inside their throats at birth,
A hand they bit because it fed them,
Two rats from a ship that is still sinking,
A collection of various split hairs,
The leaf they turned over too late.

Melt the spoons into a key
And the house you sought will appear.
Set your supper on the palm of your hand.
The rats will bring embers in their eyes.
The hairs will be your shepherd's flutes.
The leaf will bear their whimper
To the east and then to the west.

*

All that salt cast over the shoulder,
All that meat travelling under the saddles of nomads. . .

Here comes a forest in wolf's clothing,
The wise hen bows to the umbrella.

When the bloodshot evening meets the bloodshot night,
They tell each other bloodshot tales.

That bare branch over them speaks louder than words.
The moon is worn threadbare.

I repeat: lean days don't come singly,
It takes all kinds to make the sun rise.

The night is each man's castle.
Don't let the castle out of the bag.

Wind in the valley, wind in the hills,
Practice will make this body fit into bed.

All roads lead
Out of a sow's ear
To what's worth
Two in the bush.

# THE TALE

Put down the pen
and go to sleep in your chair.
The only movement now
is the slow unfolding of a tale
like a white cloth
over the bare, carefully scrubbed
table of the night.

Perhaps, the instant
you close your eyes
you'll see a horse
grazing in the snow.

If you are very attentive,
you'll be able to calculate
the degree of his stillness
by the angle of his mane
in the wind.

Don't be afraid. The chair
is still hard against your back
and the cigar hasn't yet gone out
in the ashtray.

Soon, he'll move on,
for now comes that moment
in every tale when only
the shadows linger behind,

and the pond
in the woods
is like the blade of a knife
one can see through.

\*

## INVENTION OF THE KNIFE

Its blade imagined by the hanged man
in that split of a second as he glimpses
with raised eyes the rope for the last time

yields itself to his executioners
who then go home at daybreak
over the snow that makes no sound
to cut the bread fresh from the oven.


\*

## INVENTION OF THE INVISIBLE

And always someone's missing
and the light left for him in the window
is now the oldest one on earth
and still each day his shirt, bowl and spoon
are washed by his mother and sister
and the front door is unlocked just before nightfall
because that's the time
when the ones who have been gone so long
like to return

but nothing happens
although we heard his messengers
behind the wall
and yet, when we go looking for them
there's only his empty chair
around which the old ant,
now barely able to move
has almost made a circle.

## INVENTION OF THE PLACE

The door opens half-way.
The street-lights are on,
their gold barely visible
against the blue of the dusk.

Two uniformed men
stroll along the empty streets,
solemn and slow
they advance, stopping
to look in shop-windows,
into parked-cars.

One of them wears a brass whistle,
the other hides a gun with a silencer.

There's no one left on the earth.

*

INVENTION OF A COLOR

Already it's thousands of years old.
Who can say its name?
Neither black nor white.
No one sees it twice.

How strangely everything is soaked in it:
that finger straining to lift itself and that face.
Even the trees and the animals are still,
that is to say, if there were any here.

This color announces a visitor.
Somewhere no doubt a door has been opened.
It is a color of waiting, color of patience.
No one comes. It is a color of an idea
which will not complete itself in our lifetime.

The more I speak about it, the more
I realize that it doesn't exist,
like the steady dripping of a faucet
which, all of a sudden, has ceased.

## INVENTION OF THE HAT

Then the wind was a charm
against silence
tucked under the pillow
in that mute hour before sunrise
when the stars are like all that remains of the wine
in the glasses on the wedding-table,

something was hovering above the earth,
a cloud from another planet
hollowed-out where a comet slept,
tied together now in mourning with a black band.

The one who was about to shut his eyes
reached and pulled it down
over the bottle standing on his forehead,
over the jack-of-diamonds behind his left ear,
over his cigarette and his prophet's beard.

Now the secrets known only to that hat
drift on
into the troubles of a new day.

*

## INVENTION OF NOTHING

I didn't notice
while I wrote here
that nothing remains of the world
except my table and chair.

And so I said:
(for the hell of it, to abuse patience)
Is this the tavern
without a glass, wine or waiter
where I'm the long awaited drunk?

The color of nothing is blue.
I strike it with my left hand and the hand disappears.
Why am I so quiet then
and so happy?

I climb on the table
(the chair is gone already)
I sing through the throat
of an empty beer-bottle.

*errata*

Where it says snow
read teeth-marks of a virgin
Where it says knife read
you passed through my bones
like a police-whistle
Where it says table read horse
Where it says horse read my migrant's bundle
Apples are to remain apples
Each time a hat appears
think of Isaac Newton
reading the Old Testament
Remove all periods
They are scars made by words
I couldn't bring myself to say
Put a finger over each sunrise
it will blind you otherwise
That damn ant is still stirring
Will there be time left to list
all errors to replace
all hands guns owls plates
all cigars ponds woods and reach
that beer-bottle my greatest mistake
the word I allowed to be written
when I should have shouted
her name